The MIRACLE MORNING for SALESPEOPLE

COMPANION GUIDE

The Fastest Way to Take Your SELF and Your SALES to the Next Level

Hal Elrod & Ryan Snow

With Honorée Corder

THE MIRACLE MORNING FOR SALESPEOPLE COMPANION GUIDE
Hal Elrod

Introduction

Welcome to The Companion Guide for The Miracle Morning for Salespeople. The Miracle Morning for Salespeople was never meant to be a book that you would read only once and place on your shelf to collect dust. So many of us fly through dozens of self-help books in a year, but we don't always spend the time to digest the lessons, complete the exercises, and implement what we learned at a high level. This companion guide is designed to help you do just that.

Though this guide was not part of the initial plan, so many readers reached out asking for me to develop a workbook. I've built this specifically for you! It's always a no if you don't ask, so thank you for asking.

When I think back on my transformative journey of implementing the Miracle Morning in my life, I recall that it was not the book, itself, that was life changing. What made such a tremendous impact was that I actually applied all the teachings. The habits I formed became the scaffold for additional positive habits that have transformed both my life and business.

This companion guide will take you time to complete. It is not meant to be finished in one sitting. Commit to spending a part of each day working through the exercises. Schedule time each week to review what you have completed and look for ways to improve yourself and new ideas to implement. You will find that your success is in the process.

You are about to embark on an amazing journey to outline an improvement plan to build the life and business of your dreams. Take a moment right now to feel the pride and excitement that comes from choosing to make this commitment.

As you work your way through this companion guide, please look to others for support and suggestions at **www.MyTMMCommunity.com** and request to join the Miracle Morning Community on Facebook. There, you will be able to connect with like-minded individuals who are already practicing *The Miracle Morning*—many of whom have been doing it for years — to get additional support and accelerate your success.

If you are interested in additional training and coaching for yourself or your sales team, check out the coaching and seminar options at www.explosivesalesgrowth.com or email Ryan Snow at explosivesalesgrowth@gmail.com.

Let's get to work!

Table of Contents

Table of Contents

Chapter 1

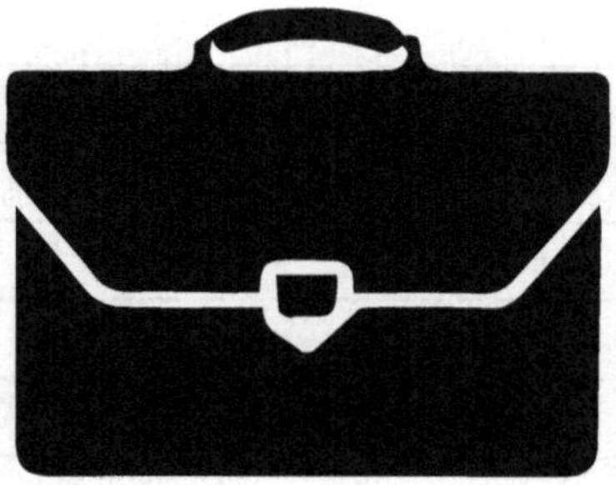

Why Mornings Matter

(More Than You Think)

Notes

CHAPTER 1

Why Mornings Matter

(More Than You Think)

How you begin each morning creates your mindset and the context for the rest of your day. If you start every day with a purposeful, disciplined, growth-infused, and goal-oriented morning, you're virtually guaranteed to crush your day.

Here are several key advantages to starting your day better:

- You'll be more proactive.
- You'll anticipate problems and head them off at the pass.
- You'll plan like a pro.
- You'll have more energy.
- You'll gain early attitude advantages.

Those are advantages. Now let's consider the challenges. The hardest part about getting up an hour earlier for your Miracle Morning routine is the first five minutes. This is the moment of truth, and the decision you make right then will change your day, your sales, and your life.

What would it take for you to be excited to get up in the morning? What benefit do you need to know you will acquire to actually make you take action? What goal would you need to achieve?

We have two aims as human beings: to seek pleasure and to avoid pain. Often the desire to avoid pain is far greater than the desire to seek pleasure because pain is typically immediate and pleasure is often delayed The question above helps you focus on the pleasure required to overcome the pain of getting up early.

Why Mornings Matter
(More Than You Think)

Now flip that question around to consider the pain of never achieving that goal? What if you hit the snooze button today and, because of that decision, you missed an opportunity that caused you to fall short of your hopes, dreams, and potential? What would that pain look like?

MORNINGS MATTER.
THEY SET THE TONE FOR THE NEW DAY.

Chapter 2

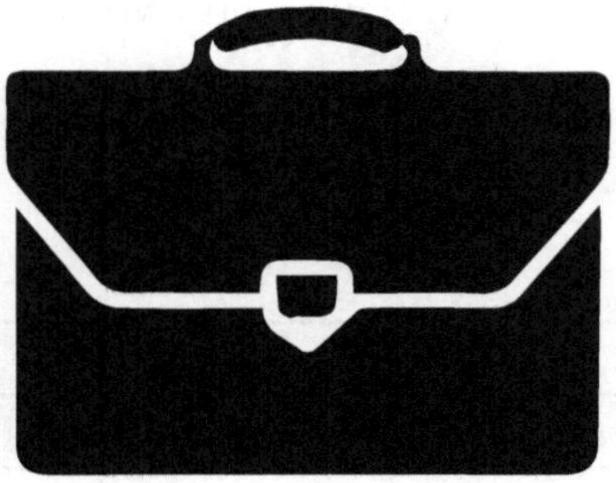

It Only Takes Five Minutes To Become a Morning Person

It Only Takes Five Minutes to Become a Morning Person

Five Steps to Waking Early:

1 Set Your Intentions before Falling Asleep

Your last thought before closing your eyes matters. Think about how you felt on Christmas Eve when you were a child. How excited were you to jump out of bed the next morning? You woke up without an alarm ready to go. Your ability to get out of bed is connected to the story you told yourself the night before about the next day and how excited you were for it.

The opposite is also true. When your last thought is, "Oh my God, it's midnight. I have only six hours to sleep. I'm going to be so exhausted tomorrow." Guess how you are going to feel the next morning?

What is your bedtime affirmation going to be? What will it take to make you want to jump out of bed tomorrow morning?

2 Move Your Alarm Clock Across the Room

This may seem obvious, but getting out of bed and moving your body will make you far less likely to hit the snooze button and go back to sleep. This one little step will increase your Wake-Up Motivation Level (WUML).

Take out your phone and set your alarm for one hour earlier than you usually get up right now!

I am committed to waking up at ________________ for the next 30 days!

It Only Takes Five Minutes to Become a Morning Person

3 Brush Your Teeth

With the Miracle Morning practice, you are creating a pattern of daily habits. You want to associate your alarm going off with an immediate series of steps you take. This is a simple step that is easy to complete and will get you past another threshold in your WUML.

What other simple thing could I do to keep me out of bed and make part of my routine?

____

____

____

____

____

____

____

____

4 Drink A Glass of Water

After six to eight hours without water, your body will be mildly dehydrated. Dehydration creates fatigue. Often, when people feel tired and want to sleep longer, what they really need is more water.

I currently drink ___________ ounces of water per day.

I am committed to drinking ___________ ounces of water when I wake up in the morning and an additional ___________ ounces throughout the day to stay hydrated and energetic.

5 Get Dressed or Jump in the Shower

Option 1: Lay out your exercise clothes at night on or next to your bed or just sleep in them. You will be ready to jump right into your Miracle Morning routine.

Option 2: Take a shower. I shower after my morning routine, but some people use the shower to help them wake up. If that's the case, try standing under cold water at the end. You can with a very short amount of time, like 10 seconds, and then build to a minute or so. It wakes you up, and I have read that there are additional health benefits.

Which option will you choose to start your day? ______________________________

These five steps will create momentum to start your Miracle Morning. The next chapter will walk you through what to do once you are up. I want to address one more thing before I move on though. How do you make sure these new daily routines last? Check out the next page!

It Only Takes Five Minutes to Become a Morning Person

Incorporating a new habit requires an adjustment period—don't expect this to be effortless from day one. You need to stick with it. The seemingly unbearable first few days are only temporary. While people debate about how many days it takes to form a habit, thirty days is enough to test-drive your new morning routine. People starting a new habit often experience the following phases.

Phase One: Unbearable

Phase one is when any new activity requires tremendous effort. You are trying to overcome past behaviors that have become who you are for years. Think about the soreness and discomfort from the first few days with a new exercise routine. The best thing you can do is stick with it and allow the discomfort to pass.

Visualize your first ten days. What are the obstacles that will stand in the way of your new morning routine? How will you overcome them?

Phase Two: Uncomfortable

In Phase two, your body and mind become acclimated to waking up earlier. It's still not a habit, and it may not feel like who you are. It's still a bit unnatural. The biggest temptation at this point is to reward yourself by taking a break, especially on the weekends. It's important to stay committed to developing the habit during phase two.

As you begin to become more comfortable and confident in the routine, how will you remain committed to your goal? How will you reward yourself when you reach 30 days?

It Only Takes Five Minutes to Become a Morning Person

Phase Three: Unstoppable
Phase three is where the magic happens. You will have acclimated to your new routine. These next ten days are important to cement the habit in your daily life. You should see some great results from your new habit already.

Special note: A side benefit of implementing the Miracle Morning routine consistently for 30 days is that you can use the same steps to add other, supportive habits to your day.

How do you feel now that you have built your positive morning routine habit? What is the next habit you would like to develop? What positive effects will this habit have on your life and your sales?

Notes

Chapter 3

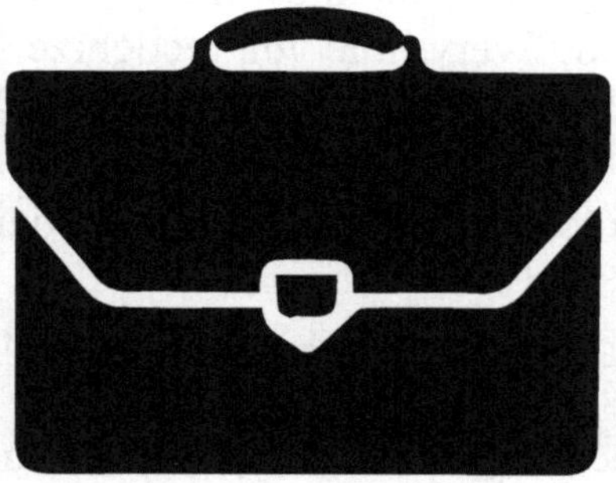

The Life S.A.V.E.R.S.

The Life S.A.V.E.R.S.

Silence

Silence is a key habit for salespeople. If you're surrounded by an endless barrage of phone calls, emails, sales meetings, tracking sheets, and pending deals that make up a life in sales, then this is your chance to stop and breathe.

Silence can take the form of meditation, prayer, reflection, deep breathing, or gratitude. You may want to incorporate a combination of these. You will be amazed by the positive physical, mental, and spiritual effects of daily silence.

Special Note: Many salespeople have trouble quieting their minds when they initially start a meditation practice. If you struggle with quieting your mind, know that you are not alone and that it is a skill that you can cultivate. Think of it like a pushup. Every time you recognize a thought and let it go, you strengthen your mind by building the habit of silence.

What specific form of silence do you feel most comfortable practicing? ____________________

I will commit to 10 minutes of ______________________ everyday for the next 30 days.

What do you hope to gain from practicing silence? What will success look like for you in practicing silence daily?

____

____

____

____

____

____

____

What obstacles do foresee disrupting your practice of some form of silence? What will you do to overcome those obstacles and build the habit of silence.

____

____

____

____

____

____

____

The Life S.A.V.E.R.S.

Affirmations

It can be difficult for salespeople to maintain confidence and enthusiasm, not to mention motivation, during the roller coaster ride of the sales cycle. Chances are, your current mindset is something you adopted without conscious thought.We have all been programmed to think, believe, act, and talk to ourselves a certain way. When we experience stress, we revert to our habitual mindset. Daily affirmations can turn this around.

So, how can you use affirmations to increase sales? If you want better sales, you need better mental programming. Affirmations are a tool for doing just that. By repeatedly telling yourself who you want to be, what you want to accomplish, and how you are going to accomplish it, your subconscious mind will shift your beliefs and behavior. Science has proven that affirmations, when done correctly, are one of the most effective tools for quickly becoming the person you need to be to achieve everything you want in your life.

Here's the catch. The old way of doing affirmations is the wrong way. Lying to yourself will not work. Your subconscious mind knows when you are being a false prophet.

I am a millionaire. No, you're not.

I have 7 percent body fat. No, you don't.

I have achieved all my goals for this year. No, you haven't.

Instead, there is a simple four step process to create effective affirmations. Affirmations written and spoken following this formula will help you to not only improve your mindset, but they will also change your behaviors and make it easier to stick to positive habits and activities.

4 Steps to Effective Affirmations

1. Start with the extraordinary result you are committed to and why.
2. Follow with the necessary actions you are committed to taking and when.
3. Recite your affirmations every morning with emotion.
4. Constantly update and evolve your affirmations.

Examples:

I am committed to doubling my income in the next 12 months, from $__________ to $__________, so that I can provide financial security for my family.

OR

I am 100 percent committed to losing __________ pounds and weighing __________ pounds by ______________(date), so I have more energy and set an example of health and fitness for my kids.

The Life S.A.V.E.R.S.

Create affirmations in each of the major areas of your life (finances, health, happiness, relationships, parenting, etc.) and constantly update them as you learn and grow.

Start by writing your first five affirmations on the lines below following the steps above.

Visualization

Daily visualization, in addition to your affirmations, will turbocharge the programming of your subconscious mind. You will begin to live in alignment with your ideal vision and make it your reality.

When you visualize what you want, you stir up emotions that lift your spirits and pull you toward your vision. Living the excitement of your future before it arrives will create the mental fortitude to carry out the activities to reach your goal.

3 Steps for Effective Visualization

1. Get ready: Eliminate as many distractions as possible, choose some background music, sit up straight, close your eyes, clear your mind, and prepare to visualize.

2. Visualize what you really want. See yourself achieving your goal. How does it feel? What emotions come over you? Feel everything. Try to incorporate all your senses. Who is with you? What sounds do you hear? What do you see?

3. Visualize who you need to be and what you need to do to achieve what you really want. While it's great to celebrate all your victories, it's just as important to picture overcoming any obstacles or adversity along the way. What could possibly stop you from reaching your goal? Picture yourself taking the steps to overcome those obstacles.

The Life S.A.V.E.R.S.

Write out your visualization. What is your end result? What does it look, feel, smell, and sound like? Who is with you? Now write out the things that come up along the way. What obstacles will you overcome? How does it feel when you overcome adversity to push onward to your goals?

(E)xercise

Everyone knows that exercise will improve your health and increase your energy. Often we have grand plans for joining a gym or running a 10K, but most people quit before gaining traction. While exercising for 10 minutes is not that difficult and can provide impressive results, it is easier to make excuses about why you cannot exercise. The two most popular are *"I don't have time."* and *"I'm too tired."* You can overcome both of those by incorporating exercise into your morning routine and getting it out of the way before the day wears you down.

Exercise in the morning increases blood flow and oxygen levels to vital parts of your body (including your brain), releases endorphins that will improve your mood, and your overall energy. Looking, feeling, and acting more energetic and enthusiastic will carry over into your client interactions and boost your sales.

The Life S.A.V.E.R.S.

Note: If you are already a health nut or gym aficionado, and you have a workout schedule that works for you in the afternoon or evening, I'm not suggesting you rearrange your entire schedule. Just add a few minutes of intentional movement or exercise to kick-start your morning.

What are three benefits you expect to gain from adding exercise to your routine?

____

____

____

In what areas do you hope to improve physically?

____

____

____

On a scale from one to ten where would you rank your current health and fitness? What would it take to increase that rating by one? What would a ten look like for you?

____

____

____

____

What type of exercise will you commit to doing everyday? What is your exercise game plan?

____

____

____

What might stop you from exercising daily? What will you do to overcome those obstacles?

____

____

____

The Life S.A.V.E.R.S.

Reading

One of the fastest ways to achieve everything you want is to model successful people. For every goal you have, an expert out there has already achieved it or something similar. And, as Tony Robbins has said, “Success leaves clues.”

Want to be a multi-millionaire salesperson? Looking to build better relationships with clients? Do you want to generate more referral business? Hoping to take your sales skills to a level ten?

There are plenty of books in addition to this one written by those who have achieved super sales success. Here are some of my favorites:

On Selling:

High Trust Selling by Todd Duncan
Influence by Robert B. Cialdini
The Sales Bible by Jeffrey Gitomer
The 10X Rule by Grant Cardone
7L: The Seven Levels of Communication by Michael J. Maher
The Greatest Salesman in the World by Og Mandino
The SPEED of Trust by Stephen M.R. Covey
Go for No! by Richard Fenton and Andrea Waltz

On Mindset:

The One Thing by Gary Keller and Jay Papasan
The Game of Life and How to Play It by Florence Scovel Shinn
The Compound Effect by Darren Hardy
Taking Life Head On by Hal Elrod
Think and Grow Rich by Napoleon Hill

In addition to finding sales success, you can transform your relationships, increase your self-confidence, improve your communication or persuasion skills, learn how to become healthy, and improve any other area of your life you can imagine.

What areas will you look to improve during your Miracle Morning?

The Life S.A.V.E.R.S.

Use this space to develop a reading list as you progress with your Miracle Morning routine.

Rereading good personal development books is an underused yet effective strategy. Rarely can you read a book once and internalize all of the value from that book. Achieving mastery in any area requires repetition.

What three books will you read at least four times this year? What do you hope to gain from each of them?

Book 1: ____________________

The Life S.A.V.E.R.S.

Book 2: ____

Book 3: ____

The Life S.A.V.E.R.S.

The Miracle Morning For Salespeople Reading Memory Jogger

Book Title: ______________________________________

Author: ____

Key Lessons:

Favorite Quotes:

Action Plan:

The Life S.A.V.E.R.S.

S cribing

The scribing element of your Miracle Morning enables you to document your insights, ideas, breakthroughs, realizations, successes, and lessons learned, as well as list any areas of opportunity, personal growth, or improvement. Use your journal to note your sales strengths, what went right in each day's sales calls and meetings, and add any areas of improvement to work on later.

Your journal should allow you to do four things:

1. Gain Clarity: Writing out your thoughts and questions will help you to gain clarity.

2. Capture Ideas: Record and expand upon your ideas from reading or experiences.

3. Review Lessons: Remember and apply what you read. Writing the ideas down is the first step. Then you read and review.

4. Acknowledge Your Progress: Show gratitude and celebrate improvements. Sometimes we forget how far we've come. Your journal will help you keep track.

Sample Journal Entry

Today I am extremely grateful for my wife. She has been sick this week, which has left me in charge of getting everything ready for my three kids. Clothes, lunches, homework, baths, etc. I always knew she was an amazing mother, but this week has been an excellent reminder of just how hard she works.

My main realization this week has come from my sales appointments. I have one client whom I've not been able to move forward. They are extremely interested and show all sorts of buying signals, but there is an underlying objection. I found it through listening and putting their needs and wants before my own. We've now agreed to move forward on a specific date in the future, and we're taking the initial steps now. Had I pushed on my own agenda I may have lost them as a client. By staying in curiosity and digging deeper, they now see me as being on their side as a trusted advisor because I worked to make it work for them.

I listened to a podcast on the power of the calendar this morning. Though I'm already a strong proponent and avid practitioner of time-blocking, I learned some helpful tips around the importance of committing to and protecting that time. One area where I've struggled and continue to work on is being present in the moment. I often think about or work on two or three things at the same time, or I'm not completely present with my family when I'm home. By protecting the time blocks and being as effective and productive as possible during those times, I allow myself the freedom to do the same during my family time blocks at home.

The Life S.A.V.E.R.S.

Scheduling Time to Review Your Journal Entries

While writing down your thoughts, ideas, and insights can be a powerful exercise on it's own, the real growth comes in reviewing your journal entries. In the next section, I will cover time -blocking. I highly recommend that you schedule a session each week to review your entries for the upcoming week. I also recommend that you set one hour every month to review all of your entries from that month.

Look for anything that stands out. What did you accomplish this month? Is there a great insight you had from reading or reviewing your progress that you should make a note of? Do you see certain thought patterns, good or bad, regularly? Do you notice anything that may be holding you back from achieving a goal? Is there something you keep committing to but not actually doing? What do you need to do to take the next step? What can you do right now? Today? This week?

Take five to ten minutes to complete a journal entry below. If you are not sure what to write, answer some of the questions above.

30 Day Challenge

We challenge you to implement the Miracle Morning routine for 30 days to begin the journey of growing your self and your sales. Implement each of these six habits daily and keep track of how you and your business change during the process. We have included pages at the end of the workbook to help you keep track of your 30-day challenge.

Now let's dive into the Not-So-Obvious Selling Principles! Feel free to complete the next couple sections as part of your Miracle Morning routine.

Chapter 4

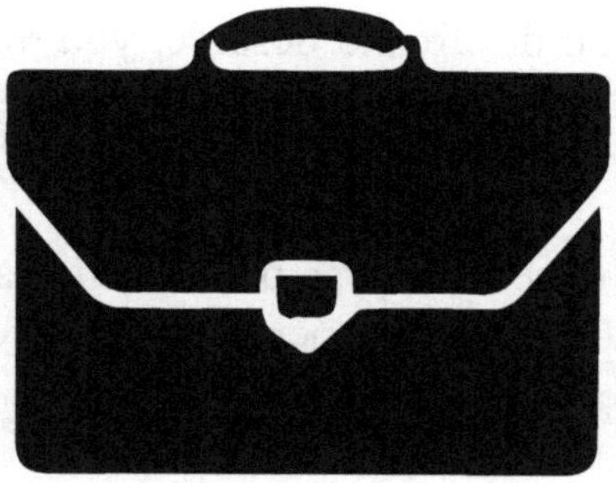

Not-So-Obvious Selling Principle #1
Self-Leadership

CHAPTER 4

Not-So-Obvious Selling Principle #1: Self-Leadership

You're a salesperson, so you know how hard it is to sell others on something if you aren't sold on it yourself.

Salespeople are problem solvers. Your job is to help people solve their problems by presenting them with effective, and often customized solutions. If you don't believe a product or service is up to the job, it's impossible to sell it.

What you may not realize though is that as a salesperson you are also a leader. You're leading your prospective customer to make the best buying decision by guiding them through your selling process. And just as it's impossible to sell something if you don't believe in it yourself, it's impossible to lead others if you don't know how to effectively lead yourself.

To find the happiness and success you desire and deserve, you must master the key principles of self-leadership. To grow your sales, in other words, you need to grow yourself.

A Note On Mindset:
Before diving into the core principles of self-leadership, we need to address the important role that mindset plays in developing yourself as a leader and a salesperson. There are three very specific steps we can take to improve mindset on a daily basis.

1. Rephrase limiting beliefs as powerful questions.
2. See yourself as your greatest potential.
3. Actively seek support.

In the following exercises you will personally track and outline opportunities to develop your mindset into that of a top performer. Come back to these exercises regularly and consider adding these questions to your daily scribing.

Exercise: Rephrase Limiting Beliefs into Powerful Questions

When you catch yourself making a statement in the form of a limiting belief, you can use the opportunity to turn it into a powerful question that will provide useful answers and options that you might otherwise overlook.

> ***Example:*** When you say things like, *"I don't have enough time"* or *"I could never do that,"*, you could instead ask yourself, *"How could I create more time in my schedule?"* or "*How could we do that?"*

Once you ask the question, sit in silence for a few minutes and see what answers come to you.

On the next page write down three limiting beliefs. Change them into powerful questions. Jot down any ideas that come from asking the questions and leaving yourself space to answer.

Not-So-Obvious Selling Principle #1:
Self-Leadership

Limiting Belief:

Powerful Question:

Ideas for Solution:

Limiting Belief:

Powerful Question:

Ideas for Solution:

Not-So-Obvious Selling Principle #1:
Self-Leadership

Limiting Belief:

Powerful Question:

Ideas for Solution:

Exercise: See Yourself As Your Greatest Potential

As Hal wrote in The Miracle Morning, most of us suffer from Rearview Mirror Syndrome. We limit our current and future results based on who we were in the past. To avoid the pitfalls of this condition, remember this statement: *Where you are is a result of who you were, where you go depends entirely on who you choose to be from this moment forward.*

Last year's sales numbers do not tell the story of who you will choose to become this year. You may not even recognize yourself or your business in five to ten years. You have so many opportunities to learn and grow each day.

We always overestimate the change that will occur in the next two years and underestimate the change that will occur in the next ten. Don't let yourself be lulled into inaction.
(Bill Gates) from his book, The Road Ahead (Penguin Books, 1996).

Use this opportunity to dream with unlimited opportunity about who you will become. If anything is possible, who are you and what does your life look like in five years? What about in ten years?

Use the next two pages to write your answers.

CHAPTER 4

Not-So-Obvious Selling Principle #1: Self-Leadership

In five years

Not-So-Obvious Selling Principle #1:
Self-Leadership

In ten years

CHAPTER 4

Not-So-Obvious Selling Principle #1: Self-Leadership

Exercise: Actively Seek Support

Self-leaders know that they need a team to provide the support to get things done. You might need administrative support, for example, so you can do what you do best: close sales! You may need accountability support to overcome your tendency to procrastinate. We all need support in different areas of our lives, and a great self-leader understands that and uses it to her benefit. Ask yourself these questions to determine what you need from your team and who may provide it.

Who currently supports me in achieving my sales goals? How have they been effective? What is my return on investment?

If I were to add any additional form of support what would it be? How would I describe this person, and what would I want them to provide for support?

By when am I committed to add this support? ____________________

How will I measure the success of this support? How will I know it is working? How long do I expect before I notice a return on my investment?

CHAPTER 4

Not-So-Obvious Selling Principle #1: Self-Leadership

The 5 Core Principles of Self-Leadership

The following are the 5 Core Principles of Self-Leadership discussed in the The Miracle Morning for Salespeople. I want to touch on each of them briefly and also offer some exercises that will help you create an action plan for improvement in each category. You will need to commit to developing in each of these areas as part of your Miracle Morning routine.

1. Take 100 Percent Responsibility
2. Become Financially Free
3. Put Fitness First
4. Systematize Your World
5. Commit to Your Process

In the following exercises you will personally track and outline opportunities to develop your mindset into that of a top performer. Come back to these exercises regularly and consider adding these questions to your daily scribing.

Principle 1: Take 100 Percent Responsibility

Here's the hard truth: If you are not achieving the life you want right now, it's all on you.

The sooner you take ownership of that fact, the sooner you'll move forward. This isn't meant to be harsh, but the most successful salespeople in the world are rarely victims. In fact, one of the reasons they are successful is that they take absolute responsibility for each and every single thing in their lives, whether it's personal or professional, good or bad, their job or someone else's.

Hal taught me something as my coach that shifted my entire paradigm:

"The moment you take 100 percent responsibility for everything in your life is the same moment you claim the power to change anything in your life. You must understand that responsibility is not the same thing as blame. Blame determines who is at fault for something; responsibility determines who is responsible for improving a situation. It rarely matters who is at fault; what matters is that YOU are committed to improving your situation."

Not-So-Obvious Selling Principle #1: Self-Leadership

Exercise: Taking 100% Responsibility

What is an area of your business or personal life where you have been unhappy? Why is it happening? Have you been placing blame on an outside source or cause? How could you personally take control by doing something to improve the situation?

Remember: We only control ***our*** thoughts, ***our*** words, and ***our*** actions.

Principle 2: Become Financially Free

The average person has less than $10,000 in savings and an average of $16,000 in unsecured debt. Regardless of your current income, it is important that you start creating the correct mindset around money. We all need to form positive daily habits around our finances the way we do around our business, our physical and emotional wellness, and our relationships.

You've probably heard of the concept of paying yourself first. I challenge you to ask yourself, not whether you have heard the advice before, but whether or not you are acting on it.

Not-So-Obvious Selling Principle #1:
Self-Leadership

"If you won't save a dollar when you have ten, then you wont save a thousand when you have ten thousand." The habit is more important than the number.

What would it take for you to set aside 10 percent of your pay each week? Would you even notice if it were deposited automatically into a separate account you couldn't touch? What would you have to give up?

In his book Money: Master the Game, my friend Tony Robbins asks readers to complete several exercises to determine what it would cost to pay their bills every month.

Consider this for yourself. What would it cost if you added money for travel, the car and home you want? To be able to eat where you want? Finally, what would be required monthly to have everything you've ever dreamt of? (Keep in mind, you don't need to buy everything. Sometimes you need things for a brief period of time.)

What are your basic monthly expenses for your current lifestyle?

What would it cost to fund the life of your dreams?

Not-So-Obvious Selling Principle #1:
Self-Leadership

How will you fund those dreams? How much would you have to save?

How could you earn that monthly income with passive income?

Here is the key to your financial freedom. If people are compensated based on the value they bring to the world, then what is your greatest value? What do can you offer that people would pay for?

You already have the opportunity for unlimited income potential by increasing your commissions. How will you use that increase in income to grow your wealth and passive income?

If you work for a company as a sales representative, you may need to worry about only your personal expenses. If you are an entrepreneur or an independent contractor, as many salespeople are, you may need to focus your attention on your business expenses and how they affect your finances as well.

As a general rule, I suggest that you spend the majority of your business investment in the categories of leverage or lead generation and driving new business. Your profit margin and return on investment will be different depending on the particular field you work in. Find the most successful people in your field, and ask them how they invest in their own business. Use their suggestions as guidelines to manage your expenses.

IMPORTANT: Increasing profit is not always about cutting expenses. It is about holding your money accountable. When you send out a dollar, it should bring multiple dollars back to you. If it doesn't, then you need to question the validity of the expense. On the other hand, you should be careful not to stunt your business growth by failing to invest in leverage (systems, tools, and people) and lead generation (marketing and prospecting) that provides appropriate returns on your investment. The only way to calculate that return is to start by tracking results and expenses.

Not-So-Obvious Selling Principle #1:
Self-Leadership

Below you will find a basic profit and loss report, which we suggest you refine to suit your individual niche in sales. Keep in mind that tracking anything, even simplistically, is better than tracking nothing.

Income	**Goal ($)**	**Actual ($)**
Sales		
Services		
Other Income		
Total Income		
Expenses	**Goal ($)**	**Actual ($)**
Accounting		
Advertising		
Assets Small		
Bank Charges		
Cost of Goods Sold		
Depreciation		
Electricity		
Hire of Equipment		
Insurance		
Interest		
Motor Vehicle		
Office Supplies		
Postage and Printing		
Rent		
Repairs and Maintenance		
Stationary		
Subscriptions		
Telephone		
Training/Seminars		
Wages and Employment Taxes		
Total Expenses		
Profit/Loss		

Not-So-Obvious Selling Principle #1: Self-Leadership

I strongly believe that the better you manage your money and make wise decisions around your expenses, the more money you will have to manage, and the more freedom and options you will have.

Develop a Mindset of Abundance:
We tend to give things away when we have too much of it or we do not need it anymore. Giving money away provides several benefits, and creating an abundant mindset is one of them. When you give money away your financial belief system shifts from one of lack to one of abundance. If you were going to give away 10 percent of your income, where would you give it? Whom are you passionate about helping?

____

____

____

____

____

If 10 percent creates a hardship for you, and you are not able to give that amount based on your current income, then start giving some set percentage away and build the habit. As you increase your income, you can increase how much you give. If giving anything is impossible at this point, then find a way to donate your time to make a difference in the lives of others. It will help you to connect with others, feel good about your contributions to making a better world, and may increase your passion and excitement for something other than your own goals and money.

Exercise

I am passionate about helping ____.

I am committed to helping by donating ____________________ every month to help this cause. (You can complete with a donation of hours or dollars per month.)

Principle 3: Put Fitness First

I discussed exercise as part of the Life S.A.V.E.R.S., and yes, I'm going to go over it again now. The state of your health and fitness is a huge factor in your energy and success levels, especially for salespeople. Doing what's required to keep deals coming in requires a ton of energy, and sales is an energy sport. Like any sport, you need an almost endless supply of energy and stamina.

I've already mentioned the importance of tracking your results. What you focus on expands, so if you want to develop healthy habits then you need to track your behaviors (actions) and your results. On the next page there is a sample chart that will allow you to track your health habits and connect them to your sales results over time. You can feel free to create a similar chart to track your own habits. You could use actual measurements or grade on a scale of 1-10. Just make it measurable and watch for trends.

Not-So-Obvious Selling Principle #1:
Self-Leadership

Date	Ounces of Water	Servings of Fruits/ Vegetables	Servings of Whole Grains	Servings of Nuts	Servings of Fish/ Shellfish	Minutes of Exercise	Hours of Sleep Last Night	Results of Sales Meetings Today

Principle 4: Systematize Your World

Later in the workbook, I will share the sales strategies and systems I believe will be most helpful to you, but effective self-leaders have systems for just about everything, from work activities like scheduling, follow up, entering orders, and sending thank you cards to personal activities such as sleeping, eating, money, cars, and family responsibilities. Those systems make life easier, and they ensure that you are always ready to perform. What is an area that you feel your systems currently work well and help you to get things done efficiently? Describe the actual system and what makes it work.

Not-So-Obvious Selling Principle #1:
Self-Leadership

What is an area of your life where you believe you are always behind and fly by the seat of your pants and that could benefit from better systems? How much time and efficiency do you waste on these activities?

How much more could you achieve if you had all of that time back? How many more sales appointments could you make? How many more family dinners could you have? Would that be worth investing the time to build a system or find a qualified candidate to leverage that?

Not-So-Obvious Selling Principle #1:
Self-Leadership

What would your life look like if you no longer had to do that activity?

Time is likely the most important thing to systematize. If you haven't yet, you will likely reach a point in the near future where you have more money than time. Money is infinite. We can always earn more. Time on the other hand is finite. We are all gifted only a certain amount of time on this earth. Knowing that should empower us to spend our time in the best way possible, and on our ideal schedule.

Your ideal schedule will likely change as your life changes, your income changes, and you build passive income. I've included two ideal schedules to complete below. The first is your ideal schedule based on where you are today. The second is your ideal schedule five years from now. If you had complete control over your calendar, which you do, what would it look like? We suggest color-coding your calendar based on types of activity. (For example, lead generation, appointments, exercise, personal or family time, etc.) This way you can quickly tell with one glance when you need to devote more time to a particular activity.

Not-So-Obvious Selling Principle #1:
Self-Leadership

This is your ideal schedule for your life as you know it. How are you currently spending most of your time? What do you need to do more or less of?

Time	Mon.	Tues.	Wed.	Thu.	Fri.	Sat.	Sun.
4:00							
4:30							
5:00							
5:30							
6:00							
6:30							
7:00							
7:30							
8:00							
8:30							
9:00							
9:30							
10:00							
10:30							
11:00							
11:30							
12:00							
12:30							
1:00							
1:30							
2:00							
2:30							
3:00							
3:30							
4:00							
4:30							
5:00							
5:30							
6:00							
6:30							
7:00							
7:30							
8:00							
8:30							
9:00							

Not-So-Obvious Selling Principle #1:
Self-Leadership

This is your ideal schedule in 5 years. I challenge you not to be too realistic. In an ideal world, what would you want your calendar to look like? What actions would you need to take to make that happen?

Time	Mon.	Tues.	Wed.	Thu.	Fri.	Sat.	Sun.
4:00							
4:30							
5:00							
5:30							
6:00							
6:30							
7:00							
7:30							
8:00							
8:30							
9:00							
9:30							
10:00							
10:30							
11:00							
11:30							
12:00							
12:30							
1:00							
1:30							
2:00							
2:30							
3:00							
3:30							
4:00							
4:30							
5:00							
5:30							
6:00							
6:30							
7:00							
7:30							
8:00							
8:30							
9:00							

Not-So-Obvious Selling Principle #1:
Self-Leadership

Each week you should set an appointment sometime between Friday afternoon and Sunday evening to review your schedule for next week and compare it to your ideal calendar. Reflect on where you are out of alignment with your personal goals and adjust whenever possible. This regular check-in and adjustment will keep you on track with your goals.

Principle 5: Commit to Your Process

If there is a not-so-obvious secret to sales success, this is it: Commit to your process without being emotionally attached to your results. Every result that you desire - from improving your physique to increasing sales - is preceded by a process required to produce that result. When you define your process, and commit to it for an extended period of time, the results take care of themselves. There's no need to stress or worry about how a day, week, or even a month of selling goes – so long as you're committed to your process for the long haul.

When I talk about committing to the process, I often describe it as if you were using a navigation program to get somewhere. You need to know two points. Where do you want to go and where are you now? The next decision is to choose a a route from point A to point B. This is the process. If you remain committed to that route or process, you will eventually attain the result you desire. If you get off track for a little bit or slow down due to traffic or an obstacle, you simply need to check in regularly and re-calculate or adjust. Even if you arrive a little later than planned, the outcome is inevitable.

What goal would you set if you knew that you couldn't fail? What would you accomplish if you truly had faith that the outcome was inevitable simply by committing to the process? How long would you commit?

Not-So-Obvious Selling Principle #1:

Self-Leadership

Do you have a clear action plan, route, or process you are following? What is it?

Have you truly committed to the process yet? Why or why not? How will you know you are fully committed?

Keep in mind that, often times, committing to a new process involves increasing your level of self-control, discipline, and will-power. The good news is you only need to exhibit self-control long enough to develop the habit. Once something is a habit and becomes part of your regular routine, it is automated, and you know longer need to tell yourself to do it. One of the easiest ways to build a habit is to attach it to something you already do every day, so that the established habit triggers the new habit as well. By building positive habits, such as those from the Miracle Morning routine, you have a huge advantage. You can now use that routine as scaffolding to build additional positive habits. This is how we establish a process. We keep adding positive habits on top of other positive habits.

Not-So-Obvious Selling Principle #1:
Self-Leadership

What positive habits do you already complete each day that you could use as leverage to build a new positive habit? What new habit will you add?

This is the entire reason I wrote *The Miracle Morning for Salespeople*. After completing the morning routine for nearly a year, I found that I needed a way to expand the routine to help grow my business as well as improve my physical, spiritual, and emotional life. This idea of scaffolding habits forms the basis for the power of the Miracle Morning and is why it is so universal.You can implement any habit you desire by adding it to the end your Miracle Morning routine.

Notes

Chapter 5

Not-So-Obvious Selling Principle #2: Energy Engineering

Not-So-Obvious Selling Principle #2: Energy Engineering

As a salesperson, you live and die by your own steam. You eat what you kill, as they say. Most of the time if you don't sell, *you don't get paid.*

The trouble isn't that it's all up to you. It's that on some days - and I know you've had those days - you wake up, and you just don't have the energy or the motivation to hunt. To get out there on those days and face uncertainty, rejection, and disappointment is no easy task. Sales requires energy, enthusiasm, and persistence on a good day. On a bad day, you need all that and more.

Sales requires an abundance of energy. And that energy is contagious - it spreads from you to your clients and prospects like a positive virus, creating symptoms of enthusiasm and yes responses everywhere. Energy is also a vaccine against rejection and disappointment. Get enough of it, and you are almost permanently inoculated against negativity.

So, how do you generate and maintain a high level of sustainable energy, on demand?

1 Sleep Smarter

Does it seem strange that in a book about getting up early and establishing a powerful morning routine doesn't tell you to stay in bed? Research shows that most adults require seven to eight hours of sleep each night to properly heal and regenerate. While some people are born with a gene that allows them to function successfully with six hours of sleep per night, that gene is found in only 3 percent of the population.

The Miracle Morning routine is not just about waking up earlier, it's about waking up better. While I do suggest you wake up earlier to complete the Life S.A.V.E.R.S. before getting on with the rest of your day, you may need to adjust when you go to sleep at night to get the appropriate amount of sleep that your body needs.

Exercise:

For the next ten days, track your sleep, and take notes about how you feel when you get up in the morning. Be aware that sleep is not the only relevant factor. We don't live in a vacuum, but see if you can settle on a waking and rising time that works for you.

Day 1

What time did I go to bed? ______________________

What time did I wake up? ______________________

How many hours of sleep did I get? ______________________

Did I need an alarm? ______________________

What was my energy like when I woke up? ______________________

____

What was my energy like midway through the day? ______________________

____

What was my energy like at the end of my day? ______________________

____

What was my energy like before bed? ______________________

____

____

CHAPTER 5

Not-So-Obvious Selling Principle #2:
Energy Engineering

Day 2

What time did I go to bed? ______

What time did I wake up? ______

How many hours of sleep did I get? ______

Did I need an alarm? ______

What was my energy like when I woke up? ______

What was my energy like midway through the day? ______

What was my energy like at the end of my day? ______

What was my energy like before bed? ______

Day 3

What time did I go to bed? ______

What time did I wake up? ______

How many hours of sleep did I get? ______

Did I need an alarm? ______

What was my energy like when I woke up? ______

What was my energy like midway through the day? ______

What was my energy like at the end of my day? ______

What was my energy like before bed? ______

Day 4

What time did I go to bed? ______

What time did I wake up? ______

How many hours of sleep did I get? ______

Did I need an alarm? ______

What was my energy like when I woke up? ______

What was my energy like midway through the day? ______

What was my energy like at the end of my day? ______

What was my energy like before bed? ______

Not-So-Obvious Selling Principle #2: Energy Engineering

Day 5

What time did I go to bed?

What time did I wake up?

How many hours of sleep did I get?

Did I need an alarm?

What was my energy like when I woke up?

What was my energy like midway through the day?

What was my energy like at the end of my day?

What was my energy like before bed?

Day 6

What time did I go to bed?

What time did I wake up?

How many hours of sleep did I get?

Did I need an alarm?

What was my energy like when I woke up?

What was my energy like midway through the day?

What was my energy like at the end of my day?

What was my energy like before bed?

Day 7

What time did I go to bed?

What time did I wake up?

How many hours of sleep did I get?

Did I need an alarm?

What was my energy like when I woke up?

What was my energy like midway through the day?

What was my energy like at the end of my day?

What was my energy like before bed?

Not-So-Obvious Selling Principle #2:
Energy Engineering

Day 8

What time did I go to bed? ___

What time did I wake up? ___

How many hours of sleep did I get? ___

Did I need an alarm? ___

What was my energy like when I woke up? ___

What was my energy like midway through the day? ___

What was my energy like at the end of my day? ___

What was my energy like before bed? ___

Day 9

What time did I go to bed? ___

What time did I wake up? ___

How many hours of sleep did I get? ___

Did I need an alarm? ___

What was my energy like when I woke up? ___

What was my energy like midway through the day? ___

What was my energy like at the end of my day? ___

What was my energy like before bed? ___

Day 10

What time did I go to bed? ___

What time did I wake up? ___

How many hours of sleep did I get? ___

Did I need an alarm? ___

What was my energy like when I woke up? ___

What was my energy like midway through the day? ___

What was my energy like at the end of my day? ___

What was my energy like before bed? ___

Not-So-Obvious Selling Principle #2:
Energy Engineering

After tracking your sleep for ten days, what do you currently believe is your ideal amount of sleep?

One of the easiest ways to improve the quality of your sleep is to follow a schedule. When you go to bed and rise at the same time everyday, you will find that your body will settle into a natural rhythm. While not every day will go as planned, it is best to choose an ideal bedtime and waking time.

What is the ideal bedtime and waking time for your body?

Make a commitment

I commit to getting to bed at ________________, and waking up at ___________________ for the next 30 days to create a positive habit that will ensure that I get the appropriate amount of sleep to maintain energy throughout each day and help me reach my goals.

1. Rest Your Mind

Many of us confuse rest with recreation. To rest, we do things like hike, garden, workout, watch TV or even party. Any of these activities can be termed restful only because they are breaks from work, but truthfully they cannot be defined as rest.

Rest has been defined as a kind of waking sleep, experienced while you are alert and aware. Rest melts away stress, and research proves it. Resting practices like yoga and meditation also lower your heart rate, blood pressure, and oxygen consumption, and they alleviate hypertension, arthritis, insomnia, depression, infertility, cancer, and anxiety.

The spiritual benefits of resting are profound. Slowing down and getting quiet means you can actually hear your own wisdom, inner knowledge, and inner voice. And yes, in case you are wondering, you'll be more productive, nicer to your friends and family members (not to mention your prospects and clients), and in general much happier as well. Our personal batteries need to be recharged. The best way to recharge them is to simply rest.

Not-So-Obvious Selling Principle #2:
Energy Engineering

What do you currently do on a daily basis to allow yourself to rest?

What is one thing that you could implement that would improve how you rest daily? When will you start? How will you know it is working?

Some simple tips for regularly scheduled rest:

1. Meditate daily for 5-20 minutes.

2. Choose one day a week for a few hours of rest.

3. Go for a walk in nature.

4. Shut off the radio and drive in silence for part of your trip.

5. Turn off the television. Sit quietly.

6. Mindfully drink a cup of tea.

7. Read something inspirational.

8. Write in your journal.

9. Get a massage.

10. Attend a retreat. One of my most restful experiences was a silent 12 hour period during one of my retreats.

Not-So-Obvious Selling Principle #2:
Energy Engineering

Exercise:

Get out the annual calendar. Plan your longer periods for rest and relaxation before adding productivity and work. Whether you take one, two, or three vacations in a year, you need to take time for your body and mind to recharge.

Please consider what you are calling rest. Trips do not have to involve spending huge sums of money. Camping in a tent for a week with no technology can provide profound rejuvenation.

In the space provided below, write about the trips you intend to take in the next twelve months. Where will you go? What will you do or not do on these trips? How many restful activities can you include in them? Who will be with you? How will you feel during the trip and upon your return? When will you go? Block the time in your annual calendar now, or these trips will not happen. Remember, this type of rest is vital to your productivity.

Trip 1: ______________________________

Not-So-Obvious Selling Principle #2:
Energy Engineering

Trip 2: ____________________

Trip 3: ____________________

Not-So-Obvious Selling Principle #2:
Energy Engineering

3. Eat for Energy

A saleperson with low energy sells well below their potential, and when it comes to energy, food may play the most critical role of all. If you are like most people, you make your food choices based on taste first, and consequences second, if at all. There is nothing wrong with eating foods that taste good, but if you want to be truly healthy and have the energy to sell like a champion, *you must learn to value the energy consequences of the food you eat, above the taste.*

Like any other area of life, what we focus on expands. The first step to eating for energy is to pay attention to the way different foods and eating habits make us feel. I suggest adding the following exercise to your journal and completing it on daily basis.

Exercise:

What is your typical daily diet? What do you eat for breakfast? Lunch? Dinner? Do you snack throughout the day?

How do you typically feel after you eat a meal? How do you feel one hour later?

Not-So-Obvious Selling Principle #2:
Energy Engineering

Add this question to your journal and keep track for 30 days. Answer it after each meal and snack. Set a timer for one hour after eating.

How did you feel an hour after eating your last meal? How did it affect your energy levels?

I strongly suggest adding a raw, organic, and healthy meal to your day. If you already have one, congratulations, try two.

What could you incorporate into your daily eating habits to improve your energy levels?

How could you better plan your meals and snacks to improve energy throughout the day? Would that make it easier to eat for energy?

Not-So-Obvious Selling Principle #2:
Energy Engineering

Staying hydrated is one of the most important steps you can take to improve your health and increase your energy. Often when people feel tired during the day, they would do just as well to drink 16-20 ounces of water as they would to take a nap. Research shows we should consume half of our body weight in ounces of water each day. For example, if a person that weighs 180 pounds, they should consume 90 ounces of water per day on average. This is a good rule of thumb. If you have no idea how much water you drink daily, you are likely not drinking enough.

How many ounces of water do you drink daily?

What are three things you could do to ensure that you drink enough water each day?

1.

2.

3.

CHAPTER 5

Not-So-Obvious Selling Principle #2:
Energy Engineering

Full and Fair Disclosure: We are on the same journey. I have struggled with many of these same battles. My Miracle Morning routine has made me more aware of my energy and how my choices surrounding sleep, rest, and diet affect it. Though I don't like to deny myself certain foods, I have added as many healthy options to my day as possible. I have found that by increasing my intake of healthy, energizing options, I am less likely to make poor choices during a weak moment. I still eat some of what I would call 'junk food', but I do it with intent and full knowledge that it will negatively affect my energy, and I do it only when I am ok with the consequence.

After working through this chapter, what is the one habit that you are committed to changing to increase your energy? What made you choose that particular habit or activity? Once you succeed, what will you implement next?

Notes

Chapter 6

Not-So-Obvious Selling Principle #3: Unwavering Focus

CHAPTER 6

Not-So-Obvious Selling Principle #3: Unwavering Focus

Focus is the ability to maintain clarity on your highest priorities. You take all the energy that your learned to generate for yourself, zero it in on what matters most, and keep it there, regardless of what is going on around you.

When you harness the power of focus, you don't become superhuman, but you can achieve seemingly superhuman results. And the reasons why are surprisingly straight forward:

1. **Focus makes you more effective.** Being effective doesn't mean to do the most things or to do things the fastest. It means to do the right things. You engage in the activities that move the needle in your business and generate sales.

2. **Focus makes you more efficient.** Being efficient means to do things with the least amount of resources like time, energy, or money. Every time your mind wanders away from your work, you waste those things, particularly time. In sales, time is money, so every moment that your focus wavers is another dollar (or thousands of dollars) lost.

3. **Focus makes you more productive.** When you focus on your highest priorities, do the right things, and do them in the right way, you get more done with less effort. Too often we confuse being busy - engaged in activities that don't produce sales, like cleaning your car or reorganizing your leads for the 12th time this month - with being productive. By taking the steps that we are about to cover, you'll learn how to develop the habit of unwavering focus and join the ranks of the most productive salespeople in the world.

Exercise 1: Create Your Ultimate Environment for Focus

Find your best environment to focus. In your life right now, what location helps you focus your attention to be your most productive? What makes this particular place effective for you?

Not-So-Obvious Selling Principle #3:
Unwavering Focus

If you don't currently have a great environment for focus, what would it take to create one? How can you make that happen?

The best part about having an environment where you can focus is that, over time, the environment itself will trigger focused action. Do yourself a favor and create your workspace. Then use it!

Not-So-Obvious Selling Principle #3: Unwavering Focus

Exercise 2: Clear the Clutter

Make a list of everything you can think of that needs to get done today, tomorrow, this week, and this month. Write it all down.

Don't you feel better already? Holding all of those to-do items in your mind requires a ton of resources. You don't need to remember them all right now, and they do not all require your attention right now either. Write them down and free up some RAM in your brain. Two other exercises we suggest:

1.) Schedule a half-day to clean up your workspace. Organize your piles of paperwork, and throw things out.

2.) De-clutter your life. Too many physical things in your space will slow productivity. Take an hour and pick a drawer to work with. You don't have to take on the whole house in one sitting.

Not-So-Obvious Selling Principle #3:
Unwavering Focus

Exercise 3: Build Unwavering Focus

Once you identify your focus place, and begin the process of de-cluttering your life, you should experience a remarkable increase in focus simply from clearing the fog in your mind. Now it's time to take things to the next level. Use three questions to improve your focus every day.

What's working that you **should *keep* doing** (or do more of)?

What do you **need to *start* doing** to accelerate your results?

Not-So-Obvious Selling Principle #3:
Unwavering Focus

What do you **need to immediately *stop* doing** that's holding you back from going to the next level?

Exercise 4: Automate, Outsource, or Delegate

Make a list of everything you do during the course of the day.

Not-So-Obvious Selling Principle #3:
Unwavering Focus

How much of your day is spent on your top dollar, productive activities?

Which of those items could be automated? (Think online bills or email drip campaigns)

Which of those items could be outsourced? (Add a third party social media expert or house-cleaner)

Which of those items could be delegated? (Am I ready to hire someone?)

Not-So-Obvious Selling Principle #3: Unwavering Focus

Exercise 5: Time-Blocking with The Foundational Schedule

Obviously our schedules change weekly based on travel, trainings, vacations, or meetings, but creating an ideal schedule for the week makes time-blocking a simple task. Use this calendar to lay out the ideal foundational schedule for a week. Make sure you include your top dollar producing activities. Use the schedule from Chapter 4, and remove any blocks that could be systematized, automated, or delegated.

Time	Mon.	Tues.	Wed.	Thu.	Fri.	Sat.	Sun.
4:00							
4:30							
5:00							
5:30							
6:00							
6:30							
7:00							
7:30							
8:00							
8:30							
9:00							
9:30							
10:00							
10:30							
11:00							
11:30							
12:00							
12:30							
1:00							
1:30							
2:00							
2:30							
3:00							
3:30							
4:00							
4:30							
5:00							
5:30							
6:00							
6:30							
7:00							
7:30							
8:00							
8:30							
9:00							

CHAPTER 6

Not-So-Obvious Selling Principle #3:
Unwavering Focus

Time-Blocking Tips

1. Start with your ideal foundational calendar in place and move only what you must. Someone will always control your calendar, and it might as well be you.

2. Schedule a weekly one hour meeting with yourself to make any changes to your schedule and prepare mentally and physically for the week.

3. Work backwards. By preparing for the end of the week first instead of one day at a time, you won't stop before you are finished, because you will feel the pressure to be prepared for Monday.

4. Do not erase top dollar, productive activities. If unavoidable circumstances arise, which they frequently do, you must move your most productive activities to another time in your schedule.

5. Have integrity. Do what you say you' are going to do. If it is in your calendar, then you must do it.

6. If you do not have an appointment with a client during an allotted time, your job is to use that time slot to get another appointment.

Notes

Chapter 7

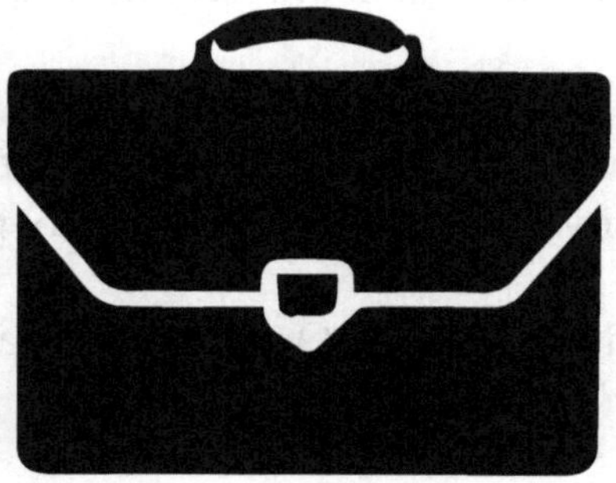

Sales Acceleration Skill #1: Attracting Level 10 Customers

Sales Acceleration Skill #1: Attracting Level 10 Customers

Not everyone is your customer. In fact, for some salespeople, hardly anyone is a customer. But those that are? They're Level 10, and they're going to transform your sales career.

But which ones are your Level 10 customers, and how do you find and attract them? Your prospects aren't walking the streets wearing "Level 10" t-shirts. You have to identify them by *qualifying* them.

Qualifying is about two things. As salespeople, we have a tendency to want to close every deal. We want to help every lead buy our product or service. However, as an economics major in college, I learned the principle of opportunity cost. In a nutshell, this means that when we say "yes" to something, we are saying "no" to something else. When we spin our wheels with an unqualified client, not only do we have the cost of a "no-sale", but we also give up the time that could have been spent with a qualified client who would have purchased.

No matter how hard you work or how many hours you put in, the great benefits of working with Level 10 clients will remain just out of reach if you aren't willing to qualify potential customers.

Fortunately, that process isn't as hard as it sounds. Qualifying is really about two things: *deciding what a Level 10 customer looks like and saying "no" to everyone else.*

Exercise 1: Focusing on Your Level 10 Prospects

Build a list of five to ten character traits that describe your Level 10 customers exactly. Think back to your best clients. What do you know about them? Attracting Level 10 customers starts with being crystal clear about who your Level 10 customer is. Once you create the list, hang it up so you can see it, and commit to this standard for prospecting.

Sales Acceleration Skill #1: Attracting Level 10 Customers

Exercise 2: Create Your Top Prospect List

List your top 50-150 prospects. Get out of your comfort zone and realize that there are hundreds of Level 10 customers in your current network just waiting for you to identify and call them. Think of everyone you know: friends, family, current clients, your database, yellow pages, professionals that you do business with, and even prospects who liked your offering, but the timing wasn't right when you first saw them. Start by making your list as long as possible, and then qualify them later. Simply write the names for now, and you can add them to your database and grab contact information later.

CHAPTER 7

Sales Acceleration Skill #1: Attracting Level 10 Customers

Sales Acceleration Skill #1: Attracting Level 10 Customers

Aside from qualifying the right people, one of the best things we can do to make our lives easier is to attract the right people to us. An invisible yet unstoppable key to success is to make yourself irresistible to others. If you feel like you're doing everything right, yet there's a block in business flowing to you, chances are the issue lies not in what you are doing, but how you are being. It's critical to be likeable and approachable.

Exercise 3: The Best and The Worst

One of the best ways to help someone see the right decision is to help them view the experience from another perspective. Take a moment and think back to your own experiences as a customer. When have you felt like a salesperson was crucial in helping you make a great decision? How did they act? What do you remember about them? What about them made you feel comfortable?

Now think back to a time when you did not resonate with a salesperson? Maybe you didn't connect, or maybe you downright loathed them. What made you feel uncomfortable? What created the disconnect? Did they need to do something differently, or was it their personality or character that bothered you?

Sales Acceleration Skill #1: Attracting Level 10 Customers

When have you found yourself acting like your first example? Have you ever found yourself acting as your second example? What was the difference? How can you correct it?

The best way to become a likeable, approachable salesperson is to rock your Life S.A.V.E.R.S. every morning. It's the gateway to having a magnetic personality, complete with unstoppable attitude, and a irresistible energy.

When you practice Silence, you create a sense of peace within, which improves your emotional intelligence and allows you to interact with people in a calmer and more thoughtful manner. Following with Affirmations develops clarity for the vision of the person you are becoming — your Level 10 self — so that you can be present to living in a alignment with your vision, every day. By clearly defining the mindset, habits, and actions that you aspire to embody, and reading them every day, you will accelerate how quickly your vision becomes reality. Visualization allows you to experience yourself being the person you just affirmed. Make sure that when you visualize, you feel what that experience will feel like.

Sales Acceleration Skill #1: Attracting Level 10 Customers

Exercise 4: A Parade of Level 10 Clients

Choose a location that makes sense for where you work: office, car, coffee shop, home, etc. Imagine that one day you are working on your prospect list. Something clicks as you are building your list, and you cannot stop writing down the names of Level 10 customer prospects that are flooding your brain. A huge smile comes over your face as you write feverishly.

Whose names are you writing? Get them down.

How does it feel as you can see yourself endlessly recording the names of so many perfect, Level 10 clients?

CHAPTER 7

Sales Acceleration Skill #1: Attracting Level 10 Customers

Go back to your vision. You have written down almost 50 Level 10 prospect names when suddenly some of the first people you had written down start emailing you, calling you, texting you, and even showing up looking to buy from you. How does it feel to have these sales manifest without effort? Why are they so excited? Why are they attracted to you? Who have you become at this point?

It's time to put a plan into action. You have worked through exercises to visualize and practice what you need to do and the person we you need to become. You have determined who you need to reach out to. Now let's create the plan for turning these prospects into clients.

Sales Acceleration Skill #1: Attracting Level 10 Customers

Exercise 5: Prospecting Plan

Set a goal for new clients from prospecting in the next 90 days.

____
____
____
____
____
____
____

Determine your top three sources of Level 10 prospects.

Source 1: ____________________

Source 2: ____________________

Source 3: ____________________

For each of the three sources, determine four or five strategies to connect with prospects and convert them to appointments or clients.

Source 1: ____________________

Strategy 1: ____________________
____

Strategy 2: ____________________
____

Strategy 3: ____________________
____

Strategy 4: ____________________
____

Strategy 5: ____________________
____

Sales Acceleration Skill #1: Attracting Level 10 Customers

Source 2: ______________________________

Strategy 1: ______________________________

____

Strategy 2: ______________________________

____

Strategy 3: ______________________________

____

Strategy 4: ______________________________

____

Strategy 5: ______________________________

____

Source 3: ______________________________

Strategy 1: ______________________________

____

Strategy 2: ______________________________

____

Strategy 3: ______________________________

____

Strategy 4: ______________________________

____

Strategy 5: ______________________________

____

If you followed this plan, could you see yourself converting enough prospects into clients to reach your goal in the next 90 days?

If not, what would you need to change in your action plan to make it happen?

Go ahead and make those changes now to ensure you can hit your goal.

These actions must be done every day to build the habit and guarantee success. There is tremendous power in prospecting with consistency and frequency. However, the other feeling you can almost always count on whenever there is consistency is monotony and boredom. It's highly likely that at some point you will wake up and decide you don't feel like it that day. That may be one of the reasons you are working through this book.

Remember these wise words from Hal:

"Salespeople who only do what they feel like doing don't do much. To be successful, you must take action even when you don't feel like it, knowing that action itself is what produces the motivation you need to follow through."

In other words, motivation doesn't create action; action creates motivation.

Notes

Chapter 8

Sales Acceleration Skill #2:
Miraculous Presenting

CHAPTER 8

Sales Acceleration Skill #2: Miraculous Presenting

I bet you have experienced a time when you knocked your sales presentation out of the park. Think back to the appointment when you left, contract and check in hand, vibrating with a sense of joy, excitement, and accomplishment, feeling like you could sell just about anything to anyone. It was a moment when all the elements of presenting your offer came together beautifully. Most salespeople see those moments as a result of good fortune, a lucky day in a string of less fortunate ones. However, the truth is that with a shift in your perspective and your approach, every presentation can progress as though buyer, product, and seller were meant to connect.

You can, in other words, make the stars align.

The Miracle Morning Approach to Presenting

Step 1: Learn It All

Step 2: Craft Your Presentation

Step 3: Practice and Rehearse

Step 4: Stand and Deliver

Step 5: Post-Presentation Review

Great sales presentations begin long before you ever meet a prospect. Even before they create a presentation, successful salespeople have built an incredible knowledge base around their product, their prospects, and their competition. The more insight you have about what you're selling and to whom you are selling it, the more comfortable you will feel, and the more effective you will be as a salesperson.

Exercise 1:

Let's break down your product, your client's needs, and your competition. You may feel like you know this information and that it is already in your presentation. Put your presentation aside and answer these questions anyway. You may be surprised by what you learn.

Part 1: Know Your Product or Service

What is your product or service?

CHAPTER 8

Sales Acceleration Skill #2: Miraculous Presenting

What are the amazing features your product offers?

How do these features benefit your client? How do they solve their problem or meet their needs?

What are the features and benefits that are unique to your product or service? What makes you stand out?

What is your company's history? How do your prospects know they can rely on you and your company in the long run?

Part 2: Know Your Customer

Pause here to reflect on some of your best clients. What makes them your best clients?

CHAPTER 8

Sales Acceleration Skill #2: Miraculous Presenting

For each of those clients, what is the problem that you solve for them?

Reach out three to five of your best clients and ask them: "As part of our constant effort to improve and offer the highest and best products and services, we would love to know two things: What do you love about our products or services that makes you keep coming back to purchase? Is there anything you would like to see us change?" Write down your responses.

Sales Acceleration Skill #2: Miraculous Presenting

Is there a group of customers you are not yet meeting whose problems you could solve? Why haven't you spoken with them yet? By when will you speak with them?

What are the top five questions you ask during your presentation in order to really get to know the individual prospects needs and wants?

1.

2.

3.

4.

5.

Is there a question you should be asking that you have not asked in the past?

____

____

____

Part 3: Know Your Competition

Knowing what you are selling and to whom, will take you a long way, but remember, you're not selling in a vacuum. There are other salespeople with great products and services who are out there trying to do the same thing that you are. Of course, they won't be as prepared as you, but that's no reason to discount them.

Who are your top three competitors?

____

____

____

Spend an hour researching your top competitors. How do their products stand up to yours? How do their features and benefits compare?

Competitor 1: ____

____

____

____

____

____

____

____

____

____

____

____

____

____

____

Competitor 2: ______________________________

Competitor 3: ______________________________

CHAPTER 8

Sales Acceleration Skill #2: Miraculous Presenting

What makes your product or service stand out from the competition?

What made you choose to sell your product or service versus your competitor's?

What could you do to improve your product or service to further distinguish yourself from your competition?

CHAPTER 8

Sales Acceleration Skill #2: Miraculous Presenting

Exercise 2: Craft Your Presentation

In the last exercise, you developed much of the material for building your presentation. Using this exercise, determine the pieces that will help your prospects say yes to your offering and become lifelong clients.

The presentation is built in 7 stages.

- Establish Rapport and Credibility
- Identify the Problem or Need
- Describe Your Solution
- Emphasize the Benefits
- Present the Price
- Close the Sale
- Ask for Referrals

Stage 1- Establish Rapport and Build Credibility

How do you currently build rapport with prospects? What questions do you currently ask?

CHAPTER 8

Sales Acceleration Skill #2: Miraculous Presenting

Keep in mind not to get too hung up on small talk. Going down the rabbit hole of personal connection may take away from the effectiveness of your sales presentation. Let them know you appreciate their time, and that you would like to ask some questions to get to know them better and see if your product or service makes sense for them. You might say, "I want to thank you so much for taking the time to meet with me. I know we are both very busy, and I want to make sure I do not waste your time." This mutual respect for each other's time will establish the beginning of rapport. It shouldn't feel forced, like small talk, and it may help them open up in answering your questions to save time.

How do you build credibility with prospects in your presentations? What types of information do you offer them?

What client testimonials do you use? How can you incorporate them to establish your credibility?

Sales Acceleration Skill #2: Miraculous Presenting

Do you have any articles or third party reports that show your product, service, or company in a positive light? How could you incorporate them into your presentation?

Stage 2 - Identify the Problem or Need

Now that we have established some rapport and built credibility with the prospect, it is time to let them do all of the talking. A great reminder for this part of the presentation is the word WAIT. WAIT stands for Why Am I Talking. Ask a question and WAIT for the answer.

Depending on your product, service, and clients, you will want to phrase these questions slightly differently so they make sense for your presentation. Keep that in mind as you answer the following.

Model Question:
When thinking about ________________, what is the one thing that keeps you up at night?

(The blank has to do with your product or service. For example, when thinking about your advertising message, what's the one thing that keeps you up at night?) Craft your initial question to find out what keeps your prospect up at night.

Sales Acceleration Skill #2: Miraculous Presenting

Model Question:
On a scale of one to ten, where would you rank your current process or solution? What would make it a (add one number to their answer)? What would it take to be a ten? Craft your scale of one to ten question for your presentation.

Now, it's time to dive deeper. As they offer you information about what it would take to solve the problem, you will need some questions to help you dive deeper. Write 5 questions you could use to further explore their needs and wants. (For example, what about ________ is important to you? How will it help you reach your goals? What would that do for your company? What would your boss think of you if you could make that happen?)

1. ______________________________

2. ______________________________

3. ______________________________

4. ______________________________

5. ______________________________

Resist the urge to get into the features and benefits or your product or service during these questions. This is all about the need of the person in front of you. This needs analysis stage provides a great opportunity to build more rapport as you learn more about your client and listen for areas where your product or service can solve their problems. This is the opportunity to ask great questions and truly listen. Remember, we were given two ears and one mouth for a reason.

People hate to be sold, and they love to buy. The information you gather helps your prospects buy. You don't need to tell them later about everything that is great about your product or service. You only need to show them how it can help solve their problems. When you can show prospects the value in how your product or service can help them with their wants and needs, they almost have to say yes. Nobody says 'no' to their own goals.

CAUTION: Not spending enough time on this section is the number one reason salespeople have trouble closing. You can offer tons of product knowledge and build a whole bunch of value, but if you cannot connect to the emotion of how your product or service can help a prospect or their company achieve their goals, it will be much tougher for them to make the leap.

Stage 3 - Describe Your Solution

In the first section of this chapter, I had you list all the features and benefits of your product or services. Now you are going to present the features of your product that are most important to each prospect based on their responses to questions asked when we worked to find their problem or need. This is your opportunity to solve the problem.

Describe what you and your product are able to do.

What is the process and timeline to solve their problem?

Remember to under promise and over deliver. Do not try to oversell. If you were thorough in your needs analysis and have shown how you can solve the prospect's problem, then you have done your job so far.

Stage 4 - Emphasize the Benefits

Take the time to create a list of reasons purchasing your product makes sense.

CHAPTER 8

Sales Acceleration Skill #2: Miraculous Presenting

While explaining all the features and benefits to the client may seem like a good idea, focus on the ones the client mentioned in the needs analysis.

People buy with emotion and justify with logic. You want to lead with stories and real life examples of how your product can solve the problems that keep our prospects up at night, so they feel compelled to say YES! You will also want to show them lots of logical reasons to purchase so they can justify the excitement you've created and feel good about their decision to buy from you.

List two stories you can share in your presentation as real life examples of your product or service solving their problem.

Story 1:

CHAPTER 8

Sales Acceleration Skill #2: Miraculous Presenting

Story 2:

Enthusiasm plays an important role in getting your prospects' attention and connecting with them. Your enthusiasm is contagious. The way you tell these stories and talk about your features and benefits will directly affect the way your prospect receives them. Your Miracle Morning routine and the Energy Engineering practices should help you to maintain your energy and enthusiasm.

CHAPTER 8

Sales Acceleration Skill #2: Miraculous Presenting

What are some strategies you can use just before a presentation to increase and maintain your energy and enthusiasm?

Stage 5 - Present the Price

Present the price for your product or service in a way that leaves your prospect with no other conclusion than "Yes, I'll take it." This may include presenting options for different packages or add-on options. I recommend sharing fees or prices at the end when you've had a chance to differentiate yourself and build value in your product or service.

What are the different options or packages you can offer to meet the needs of different clients?

How do you currently tailor your packages to client's needs based on the needs analysis?

One of the most powerful keys to optimizing your prospect's perception of price is to leverage the law of contrast. The law of contrast states that when two items are presented, one after another, the second item is always perceived in contrast to the first. This is why stores put items on sale. Is $40.00 too much to pay for a shirt? Not if it's usually an $80.00 shirt.

How can you leverage the law of contrast in presenting your price?

Your prospect's reaction to your price presentation should let you know if you are building enough value in your product or service during your valuation. If they expect your price to be higher than it is, you know you've done a good job building value. People base their purchasing decisions not on price, but on what they receive in return.

Stage 6 - Close the Sale

Ask your closing questions. Stop. Be quiet and let them buy. The next chapter is dedicated to making this step easier and more comfortable, but for now, think about how you currently close the sale.

What is the most comfortable closing question you currently use? How do you get your client to sign the order?

Sales Acceleration Skill #2: Miraculous Presenting

Stage 7 - Collect Referrals

Remember: Referrals are your potential income. The more referrals you have to call, the more potential income is available to you, just waiting for you to claim it. Learning how to generate an unlimited supply of referrals gives you unlimited potential for your income.

Five Steps to Unlimited Referrals

1. Memorize, practice, and deliver a consistent referral approach every time.

What is the script you use in order to ask for referrals?

2. Set a positive expectation for referrals at the beginning of your presentation.

If you don't plant the seed early on that you will be asking for referrals later in your presentation, not only are you setting yourself up for failure, but you are leaving it up to your customer to decide whether giving you leads is a good thing or a bad thing. Wouldn't it make sense for you to take responsibility for creating a positive expectation about the act of giving referrals than to let your prospect decide, based on their non-existent experience of referring you?

Here is an example. Please feel free to customize it.

"Bob, thank you so much for meeting with me today. I really appreciate your time and promise I'll do my best to make sure you get significant value from our time together. What I'm here to show you (or help you with or discuss or assess) is ______________, but my goal is not to try to sell you anything. If you end up liking what you see and think it's a good fit, of course we'll explore your options. But my primary goal is simply for you get so much value from our discussion today that you'd feel comfortable recommending me to anyone you think could benefit from my product, just like your colleague, Jim, recommended me to you. That's really my favorite part of what I do: Just about every person I meet with is a referral from someone I've already met, so that way it's a win-win for everyone. But, like I said, I really want to focus on how you can get as much value from our time today as possible."

How do you plant the seed early on in the presentation that you will be asking for referrals?

How would explaining that so much of your business comes from past clients and referrals help your sales?

CHAPTER 8

Sales Acceleration Skill #2: Miraculous Presenting

You haven't asked for referrals yet. You are only planting the seed. What are some other opportunities to mention referrals in your presentation without asking for anything?

3. Ask for 10-15 referrals and expect to get at least 10.

Now, the number of referrals that you ask for is somewhat arbitrary. The point is, don't hope to get referrals, expect to get them. It doesn't matter if you ask for 5,10, 25, or 50 referrals. Your results are born from your expectations. You tend to get what you expect.

How many referrals do you expect to get from each prospect? ______________________

Think about that same prospect over time. How many referrals could this person give you over time if you stay in touch with them (especially past customers)? How would that change your expectations?

What can you do to continue offering value after the sale to continue to grow your referral base?

4. Let them see you already get lots of referrals.

Social proof will help to make prospects and clients feel comfortable giving you lots of referrals. Hal carried a notebook containing pages filled with 10-15 referrals from other prospects and clients. When he asked for referrals, he would flip through to get to a blank page. Remind your prospects and clients that someone referred you to them. You can use testimonials that end with lines like "I am so glad Mary introduced us." People feel more comfortable doing something when they know other people are already doing it. This also shows the benefit of referring someone because people are happy to have met with you.

What will you incorporate in your presentation to add social proof when you ask for referrals?

5. Expect to hear 'no' and be ready for it.

What are three objections you might expect to hear from clients and prospects about giving referrals?

1.

2.

3.

Sales Acceleration Skill #2: Miraculous Presenting

How can you handle each of these objections? Where could you address them earlier in the presentation before they even come up?

Exercise 3: Practice. Learn the presentation until you could do it in your sleep.

If you havn't taken out your materials and practiced your presentation, STOP! Go get them and do it now. This exercise is only helpful if you actually do the work.

Practice the presentation with a role-play partner. Then answer the following questions.

How well do you know your presentation?

Sales Acceleration Skill #2: Miraculous Presenting

How was your energy during the presentation? Do you treat practice like it's a game?

Does your presentation meet the guidelines of this chapter? What works well? What could use some improvement?

Exercise 4: Stand (or Sit) and Deliver

Your presentation may very well be your first interaction, at least face-to-face, with your prospect. Your first impression can make or break your presentation. People like to do business with people they know, like, and trust. Make sure you optimize this first opportunity to help build a relationship. Carry yourself and speak with confidence.

What are some ways you seek to make a strong first impression at every presentation?

Sales Acceleration Skill #2: Miraculous Presenting

What are some affirmations you use to build your self-confidence?

If you are planning a demonstration as part of your presentation, make sure to practice it step-by-step. If it involves technology, make sure you test it out ahead of time. The last thing you want to do is have to apologize for things not working properly. Visual aids can be quite helpful, but remember that they are only tools in your presentation. Make sure to keep it simple so as not to overshadow your product or service.

What visual aids do you use in presenting?

What are the strongest visual images?

Sales Acceleration Skill #2: Miraculous Presenting

Where would it be helpful to cut back? Are there too many distractions?

What could you add to your presentation to make it stronger?

Exercise 5: The Post-Presentation Review

After presenting to a prospect or client, write in a journal or notebook some comments based on how your presentation went. Use this information to continue to learn and grow. Constantly hone your skills, and improve your conversion rates.

What went really well? What was the best part of the presentation?

What was one area where I could have improved? What's one thing I could do better next time?

The more presentations you do, the better you will get. If you keep making the same mistakes over and over again, though, it will drastically impede your progress. Use this as a journal entry within 24 hours after each presentation. As you continue to practice and improve, your confidence will grow and your sales will increase.

Chapter 9

Sales Acceleration Skill #3: Comfortable Closing

CHAPTER 9

Sales Acceleration Skill #3: Comfortable Closing

For salespeople and prospects alike, closing is normally the most uncomfortable part of the sales process. This is largely because all human beings are afraid of making a wrong decision, so they would rather make no decision at all.

You've reached the point where you're ready to close the sale and are in need of a concrete yes or no response from your prospect. The tension is at its peak. Feeling nervous but eager, you look your prospect in the eye, and confidently ask for the order. Hoping to hear a resounding YES, you instead get an objection: "I need to think about it." Or, "I can't afford it." Or worse "I need to talk it over with my wife (or business partner, cat, spirit guide, gardener, or anyone else who isn't in the room and didn't see your incredible sales presentation).

But what if you could minimize or even remove that tension, so that closing became comfortable, easy, and even effortless? What if you were a master at handling objections before they came up?

Exercise 1: Closing is a conversation

Think about a time when you were passionately persuasive about something outside of sales? How did that conversation go? Who were you talking with? Did they have any questions or objections? Write out that conversation here.

CHAPTER 9

Sales Acceleration Skill #3: Comfortable Closing

Understand What Objections Really Are

Let's start here. An objection is not a no.

An objection is merely a concern. It is a request for more information. You may think that what you're hearing *feels* like rejection and *sounds* like 'no'. But it isn't.

"I don't know if I can afford it," isn't 'no'.

"I'm not sure if it's a fit for me," isn't 'no'.

"I don't think I need it right now," isn't 'no'.

What your prospect is really saying in each of these cases is, "I have a concern. I don't feel comfortable saying 'yes' yet. I need more information." Your job is to know the most common objections like the back of your hand, expect to hear them from prospects, and be ready to respond gracefully and effectively to overcome them.

Exercise 2: Know the most common objections.

If you don't know the common objections, you cannot answer them. The five most common ones stem from these five questions: Do I need it? Do I want it? Do I need it now? Do I trust you? Can I afford it? In other words, objections are most often related to needs, wants, timing, trust, or money. What are the ten most common objections for your product or service?

1. ____

____

____

2. ____

____

____

3. ____

____

____

Sales Acceleration Skill #3: Comfortable Closing

4. ____

____

____

5. ____

____

____

6. ____

____

____

7. ____

____

____

8. ____

____

____

9. ____

____

____

10. ____

____

____

Sales Acceleration Skill #3: Comfortable Closing

What are some ways you could answer these objections during your presentation?

CHAPTER 9

Sales Acceleration Skill #3: Comfortable Closing

4 Methods of Closing

Method 1 – The Comfortable Close
Leave some space at the end of your presentation for the prospect to voice their opinion. "So what do you think?" If they are ready to buy, it gives them the opportunity to say so. If they have some concerns, it leaves a comfortable space for them to voice the concern, so the two of you can continue comfortably with the closing conversation.

Method 2 – Give it a Try
The second method to ask for a buying decision is to ask the person, "Why don't you give it a try?" The person is then forced to ask the question themselves: "Why don't I give it a try?" You can then reinforce this with, "And I will take care of all the details." This makes it easy: a small step rather than a giant leap to the decision will often bring somebody to 'yes'.

Method 3 – Assume the Sale
This method allows you to proceed as if you got a 'yes'. The confidence of assuming yes comes from lots of little closes along the way. If the client appears to be right there with you the whole time and is shaking their head up and down, then it's time for the next logical step. Say, "The next step in the process is this." Then describe the plan of action (such as writing up the contract, explaining when the product will arrive, scheduling the first service, etc.), and wrap up the sale just as if the person had said, "I'll take it."

This is my favorite close because it eliminates the pressure of their having to make the decision. If they weren't buying, I assume I would know by then based on their reactions and comments. If they have questions, they'll still ask, and I will answer them happily and then continue.

Method 4 – Ask for Authorization
"If you'll sign here and authorize this, we'll get started." A prospect ready to buy will sign it. If they are not ready, then they will raise more objections. Either way, you have moved them to one step closer to the sale.

CHAPTER 9

Sales Acceleration Skill #3: Comfortable Closing

Exercise 3: Ask for the order.

If you don't ask, then it's already a no. Which of the four closing methods do you feel most comfortable with? What would that dialogue look like for your product or service?

Write out the closing dialogue for your presentation with a prospect. Practice this as part of your presentation and confidently ask for their business, so you can help solve their problem.

CHAPTER 9

Sales Acceleration Skill #3: Comfortable Closing

Exercise 4: Use your Miracle Morning practice.

Visualize your closing with a prospective client. Practice this technique each morning and in the car before your appointment.

Spend 10-15 minutes, or as long as you need, to see yourself meeting with a client. Hear the conversation, feel your confidence, listen for and answer their objections, and confidently close the sale.

How does it feel when your client asks a question, and you answer with confidence? Picture them nodding their head in agreement with you. Feel the excitement when you ask the closing questions and they say YES. How do you feel? How do they feel? Are they relieved and excited that your product or service meets their needs?

Chapter 10

The Miracle Equation

The Miracle Equation

The Miracle Equation is the underlying strategy that Hal used to consistently break sales records, become one of the youngest individuals ever inducted into his company's hall of fame, and go on to become a number one best-selling author, and international keynote speaker. But it's more than that. It is the same equation that ALL top performers, the top 1 percent, have used to create awe-inspiring results, while the other 99 percent wonder how they do it.

During one of Hal's push periods when he set an extraordinary goal with only 10 of 14 days available to sell, Hal considered lowering his goal, but he remembered this comment from one of his mentors, Dan Casetta:

"The purpose of a goal isn't to hit the goal. The real purpose is to develop yourself into the type of person who can achieve your goals, regardless of whether you hit that particular one or not. It is who you become by giving it everything you have until the last moment—regardless of your results— that matters most."

Exercise 1:

Who is it that you want to become in the process of rising to the top 1 percent of salespeople? What are the traits, characteristics, and strengths you are looking to develop? Why is that important to you?

The Miracle Equation

The First Decision: Unwavering Faith

Hal realized that to achieve the seemingly impossible, he would have to make the decision to maintain unwavering faith, each and every day, regardless of his results. He knew that there would be moments when he would doubt himself and times when he would be so far off track that the goal would no longer seem achievable. But it would be those moments that he would have to override self-doubt with faith that was unshakeable.

To keep that level of unwavering faith in those challenging moments, Hal repeated what he called his Miracle Mantra: "I will ________________ (make the next sale, call 20 prospects, reach my goal) no matter what, there is no other option."

This is not new, but there are very few people who will hold on to this unwavering faith. Think about interviews with actors and actresses or athletes who made it to the top 1 percent of their industry. You'll almost always find a recurring theme. They had no plan B. They put 100 percent unwavering faith into the fact that some how they were going to make it no matter what. They had to make it. There was no other option for them.

Exercise 2: What is your Miracle Mantra?

"I will ____ no matter what. There is no other option."

Say this mantra many times throughout the day. Say this every time you think about quitting, every time someone says 'no' or tells you that it can't be done. This is your key to unwavering faith.

The Second Decision: Extraordinary Effort

When you allow your faith to go out the window, effort almost always follows behind it. After all, if you can't reach your goal no matter what, then what's the point of trying. Now that you have made the first decision to maintain unwavering faith, you must commit to extraordinary effort.

Extraordinary effort comes from reverse engineering exactly what it will take to carry you to your goal. If you are at the end of this time period, and this goal has been reached, what would you have done? What would you have needed to do?

Exercise 3: What is my Extraordinary Effort?

What is the goal you committed to in your Miracle Mantra statement?

____

____

____

The Miracle Equation

When will you commit to reaching that goal by?

____

To have reached this goal by ______________________, what would you need to do to ensure success?

The Miracle Equation

What could possibly get in your way?

What can you do now to make sure that potential obstacles don't get in your way?

The Miracle Equation

How will you use the Miracle Equation to push you forward when you feel like giving up along the way?

Congratulations! You have stepped into a whole new class of people. I mentioned at the end of the book that you have completed something most people won't. You read the whole book. By completing this workbook, you have taken the next step that even fewer people will take. So many people read through these books and do not take the time to implement what they've learned. By working through this companion guide, you have thought through the lessons, written down your action items, and committed to implementation.

Keep this workbook near you always. Use the answers to the questions to drive how you spend your time every day and move you toward your personal and business goals. You have a tremendous opportunity to combine your Miracle Morning with a commitment to master your sales acceleration skills, and use the Miracle Equation to create results.

These exercises were designed to help you take every area of your life to the next level faster than you may have ever thought possible. Miraculous salespeople weren't born that way. Like you, they committed to developing themselves and their skills to achieve everything they wanted.

You are becoming one of them already! Continue the journey with the **30-Day Miracle Morning Challenge.**

This program is based on building a set of positive habits that will allow you to develop the future of your dreams. Start by developing and mastering the six habits of the Life S.A.V.E.R.S. every day for the next thirty days. The next several pages are a place for you to track your progress in this commitment. Check each of the boxes every day, and use the notes section to mark down any struggles, great ideas, or breakthroughs that take place during your morning routine.

BONUS

Miracle Morning 30 Day Challenge

TMM 30 Day Challenge

❑ **Silence**

❑ **Affirmations**

❑ **Visualization**

❑ **Exercise**

❑ **Reading**

❑ **Scribing**

❑ **Silence**

❑ **Affirmations**

❑ **Visualization**

❑ **Exercise**

❑ **Reading**

❑ **Scribing**

❑ **Silence**

❑ **Affirmations**

❑ **Visualization**

❑ **Exercise**

❑ **Reading**

❑ **Scribing**

TMM 30 Day Challenge

- ❑ Silence
- ❑ Affirmations
- ❑ Visualization
- ❑ Exercise
- ❑ Reading
- ❑ Scribing

- ❑ Silence
- ❑ Affirmations
- ❑ Visualization
- ❑ Exercise
- ❑ Reading
- ❑ Scribing

- ❑ Silence
- ❑ Affirmations
- ❑ Visualization
- ❑ Exercise
- ❑ Reading
- ❑ Scribing

TMM 30 Day Challenge

❑ **Silence**

❑ **Affirmations**

❑ **Visualization**

❑ **Exercise**

❑ **Reading**

❑ **Scribing**

❑ **Silence**

❑ **Affirmations**

❑ **Visualization**

❑ **Exercise**

❑ **Reading**

❑ **Scribing**

❑ **Silence**

❑ **Affirmations**

❑ **Visualization**

❑ **Exercise**

❑ **Reading**

❑ **Scribing**

TMM 30 Day Challenge

- ❑ **Silence**
- ❑ **Affirmations**
- ❑ **Visualization**
- ❑ **Exercise**
- ❑ **Reading**
- ❑ **Scribing**

- ❑ **Silence**
- ❑ **Affirmations**
- ❑ **Visualization**
- ❑ **Exercise**
- ❑ **Reading**
- ❑ **Scribing**

- ❑ **Silence**
- ❑ **Affirmations**
- ❑ **Visualization**
- ❑ **Exercise**
- ❑ **Reading**
- ❑ **Scribing**

TMM 30 Day Challenge

- ❑ **Silence**
- ❑ **Affirmations**
- ❑ **Visualization**
- ❑ **Exercise**
- ❑ **Reading**
- ❑ **Scribing**

- ❑ **Silence**
- ❑ **Affirmations**
- ❑ **Visualization**
- ❑ **Exercise**
- ❑ **Reading**
- ❑ **Scribing**

- ❑ **Silence**
- ❑ **Affirmations**
- ❑ **Visualization**
- ❑ **Exercise**
- ❑ **Reading**
- ❑ **Scribing**

TMM 30 Day Challenge

❑ **Silence** __________

❑ **Affirmations** __________

❑ **Visualization** __________

❑ **Exercise** __________

❑ **Reading** __________

❑ **Scribing** __________

❑ **Silence** __________

❑ **Affirmations** __________

❑ **Visualization** __________

❑ **Exercise** __________

❑ **Reading** __________

❑ **Scribing** __________

❑ **Silence** __________

❑ **Affirmations** __________

❑ **Visualization** __________

❑ **Exercise** __________

❑ **Reading** __________

❑ **Scribing** __________

TMM 30 Day Challenge

❑ **Silence**

❑ **Affirmations**

❑ **Visualization**

❑ **Exercise**

❑ **Reading**

❑ **Scribing**

❑ **Silence**

❑ **Affirmations**

❑ **Visualization**

❑ **Exercise**

❑ **Reading**

❑ **Scribing**

❑ **Silence**

❑ **Affirmations**

❑ **Visualization**

❑ **Exercise**

❑ **Reading**

❑ **Scribing**

TMM 30 Day Challenge

- ❑ **Silence**
- ❑ **Affirmations**
- ❑ **Visualization**
- ❑ **Exercise**
- ❑ **Reading**
- ❑ **Scribing**

- ❑ **Silence**
- ❑ **Affirmations**
- ❑ **Visualization**
- ❑ **Exercise**
- ❑ **Reading**
- ❑ **Scribing**

- ❑ **Silence**
- ❑ **Affirmations**
- ❑ **Visualization**
- ❑ **Exercise**
- ❑ **Reading**
- ❑ **Scribing**

TMM 30 Day Challenge

- ❑ Silence
- ❑ Affirmations
- ❑ Visualization
- ❑ Exercise
- ❑ Reading
- ❑ Scribing

- ❑ Silence
- ❑ Affirmations
- ❑ Visualization
- ❑ Exercise
- ❑ Reading
- ❑ Scribing

- ❑ Silence
- ❑ Affirmations
- ❑ Visualization
- ❑ Exercise
- ❑ Reading
- ❑ Scribing

TMM 30 Day Challenge

❑ **Silence** ______________________

❑ **Affirmations** ______________________

❑ **Visualization** ______________________

❑ **Exercise** ______________________

❑ **Reading** ______________________

❑ **Scribing** ______________________

❑ **Silence** ______________________

❑ **Affirmations** ______________________

❑ **Visualization** ______________________

❑ **Exercise** ______________________

❑ **Reading** ______________________

❑ **Scribing** ______________________

❑ **Silence** ______________________

❑ **Affirmations** ______________________

❑ **Visualization** ______________________

❑ **Exercise** ______________________

❑ **Reading** ______________________

❑ **Scribing** ______________________

A Special Invitation From Hal

Fans and readers of *The Miracle Morning* make up an extraordinary community of like-minded individuals who wake up each day, dedicated to fulfilling the unlimited potential that is within all of us. As creator of *The Miracle Morning*, it was my responsibility to create an online space where readers and fans could go to connect, get encouragement, share best practices, support one another, discuss the book, post videos, find an accountability partner, and even swap smoothie recipes and exercise routines.

I honestly had no idea that **The Miracle Morning Community** would become one of the most inspiring, engaged, and supportive online communities in the world, but it has. I'm blown away by the caliber of our 46,000+ members, which consists of people from all around the globe, and it's growing daily.

Just go to **www.MyTMMCommunity.com** and request to join The Miracle Morning Community (on Facebook). Here you'll be able to connect with like-minded individuals who are already practicing *The Miracle Morning* - many of whom have been doing it for years - to get additional support and accelerate your success.

I'll be moderating the Community and checking in regularly. I look forward to seeing you there!

If you'd like to connect with me personally on social media, follow **@HalElrod** on Twitter and **Facebook.com/YoPalHal** on Facebook. Please feel free to send me a direct message, leave a comment, or ask me a question. I do my best to answer every single one, so let's connect soon.

Notes

Notes

Made in United States
Troutdale, OR
09/13/2024

22779996R10080